Unless She Beckons

Unless
She Beckons

—— POEMS OF ——

Dafydd ap Gwilym

TRANSLATED BY

Paul Merchant *and* Michael Faletra

redbat books
La Grande, Oregon
2018

Printed in the United States of America

First Trade Paperback Edition: March 2018

ISBN 978-0-9971549-9-3
    Library of Congress Control Number: 2018937069

Published by
redbat books
2901 Gekeler Lane
La Grande, OR 97850
www.redbatbooks.com

Text set in Minion Pro

Cover Painting by David Bell
Book design by redbat design | www.redbatdesign.com

Table of Contents

Introduction

Though almost surely spurious, one of the most evocative descriptions of Dafydd ap Gwilym, the greatest poet of medieval Wales, comes to us from a sixteenth century vicar-cum-antiquarian who heard it from an old woman, who heard it from another old woman, who had allegedly met the man himself: "He was tall and slender with loose, curly yellow hair and that full of clasps and silver rings." Quite literally an old wives' tale, this description nonetheless exerts a certain hold over anyone who reads Dafydd's work. Stepping out of what now, in our squalid post-industrial age, must surely seem like the springtime of the world, the old woman's Dafydd confronts us with his strangeness, his directness, his sense of lived realness. The yellow hair suggests a boldness and vitality, the curls suggest youthful verve, the "clasps and silver rings" a concern with adornment and thus perhaps also with subterfuge; they might even evoke, to some of us, something of a scoundrel. Even his height and build convey a wiry energy and a sense of occupying palpable physical space. The poet thus described must have left one with a definite impression. As a rough metric for characterizing the man's poetry as well, the vignette hits the mark.

The description, filtered through so many intermediaries, is of course too good to be true, but it answers the reader's very real need to actualize the voice that speaks to us so coyly and confidingly, throughout his hundred and fifty or so surviving poems. For Dafydd ap Gwilym is remarkably embodied throughout his poems, which so often find their setting not only at a particular time and place but also catch their speaker, as if unawares, in peculiarly self-reflective trains of thought. The poet is lingering outside a village, loitering in the woods for a tryst that will never happen, passing by a ruined farmstead, wandering directionless in an unexpected afternoon mist, eyeing the girls in church during the celebration of the Mass, drinking in a tavern, peering through a window, stumbling in the dark. *Mutatis mutandis,* despite the centuries and the technological gulfs that separate us, Dafydd's world is also our world, and the poses that he allows himself to strike can appear surprisingly modern.

Dafydd ap Gwilym's freshness is all the more surprising because, in many ways, he was living at the end of an era. Just a few short decades before the poet's birth in about 1320, the native Welsh princes had been brutally smashed by the English under Edward I, and Wales, after successful resistance for over two centuries, had effectively become a colony of England. In terms of poetry in Wales, the Edwardian conquest of 1283 meant that the princes were no longer available as touchstones of Welsh cultural life and, more directly, as patrons of poets. While practically every other known poet from the two hundred years before Dafydd had been able to count on princely patronage, Dafydd's poems instead depict a world in which the poet seems to lack a specific occupation. Many of Dafydd's contemporaries, such as Iolo Goch, found a new sort of poetic patronage under the Anglo-Welsh gentry. Although these young poets operated in the exciting new *cywydd* meter, which Dafydd himself would soon develop to perfection, they were largely content to modify the native traditions of elegy and military panegyric to lower-status (and sometimes even half-English) audiences while still employing a diction that hearkened back often quite consciously to the sixth-century *Gododdin*.

In terms of the literary scene in fourteenth-century Wales, then, Dafydd stood as an outlier. Although he hailed from a long family line of poets and court functionaries, he made virtue of necessity and focused his poetic eye not upon the bygone glories of an increasingly anachronistic heroic ethos but instead upon the world that the earlier courtly poets had for so long almost completely overlooked: the world of love. Despite the vogue of the theme of love in European poetry throughout the High Middle Ages, it had remained a thoroughly peripheral topic for earlier Welsh poets. A couple of twelfth-century professional bards, Gwalchmai ap Meilyr (fl. 1130–1170) and Cynddelw Brydydd (fl. 1155–1200), had praised the daughters of their princely patrons in a manner vaguely reminiscent of the Occitan *trobadors* or the French *trouvères*, but their surviving love-verses strike the reader more as rhetorical exercises and encomic flourish than as serious love poetry. Another twelfth-century writer, the "poet-prince" Hywel ap Owain Gwynedd (d. 1170), evinces a more anguished—and perhaps really more sincerely love-lorn—subjectivity, but his handful of poems were not in themselves sufficiently well-read to inaugurate a tradition of love poetry or even to stand as a significant precursor to Dafydd's work.

Given the enormous emphasis that Dafydd places upon the phenomenon of love, and given too his very cannily nuanced expression of the peculiar effects of erotic longing upon the individual psyche, we might more fruitfully compare Dafydd's poetic output with that of his more luminous fourteenth-century European counterparts: Dante (1264 – 1321), Petrarch (1304 – 1374), and Chaucer (ca. 1340 – 1400). Like Dante (and like the other poets of the Italian *stilnovist* school such as Guido Cavalcanti), Dafydd is fully committed to expressing the intensity of erotic desire and to exploring with precision the impact of erotic awareness upon the soul. And, again like Dante, Dafydd was acutely aware of the potential conflation of romantic love and the love due to God. A poem like "The Girls of Llanbadarn," in which the poet surveys various amorous opportunities while in church, might seem to make light of this tension, but other poems—like "The Star," which willfully interweaves erotic and religious imagery, or "Love's Afflic-tion," which professes to strike a more penitential tone—demonstrate that the poet was equally capable of taking this conflict very seriously.

Comparison of Dafydd to his almost exact contemporary Petrarch likewise proves useful. If we consider Dafydd's hundred or so erotic poems as constituting a sort of loose *canzoniere*, we see the Welsh poet as seriously committed as the Italian poet to exploring and cel-ebrating the multiform manifestations of love. While Petrarch's Laura may inhabit a rarefied *locus amoenus* consisting of a green meadow, a rippling spring, and, of course, a laurel tree, Dafydd's erotic pursuits find a setting equally compelling, if more varied: for Dafydd, the Welsh woodland grove (as we see in poems like "Forest Communion") becomes the ideal scene for amatory attainment.

One should say that the woodland grove or "house of leaves" is the *ideal* scene for love in Dafydd's poems in full knowledge of the fact that, in the overwhelming majority of the poems, as also in Petrarch's verse, that amatory attainment is never achieved. Dafydd ap Gwilym is, in fact, the great poet of failure, perhaps the finest one the Middle Ages produced. His poem "The Mist" is paradigmatic in this regard: the speaker's carefully arranged tryst with a willing girl in his woodland grove is thwarted by the inexorable descent of an inpenetrable bank of mist (the likes of which are not uncommon in the Welsh uplands). And though the meeting with his lover never does materialize, the erotic frustration affords the poet the opportunity to engage in a humorously virtuosic and virtuosically humorous rant against the mist itself. What began as a sort of *pastourelle* turns deftly into a parodic ode to the forces of nature, allowing the poet to showcase the power and variety of his art. In another poem, "The Fox," the speaker is again "awaiting his white girl in the wood" only to be interrupted by the otherworldly intrusion of an ungainly fox into his house of leaves; in this poem, the poet's attempts to repel the fox metamorphose into an enigmatic meditation on his own inefficacy as a lover.

In terms of the customary pose of self-deprecation his poems so frequently convey, Dafydd ap Gwilym is perhaps most like the third of the medieval luminaries mentioned above, the English poet Geoffrey Chaucer. Indeed, in many ways, Dafydd expresses in love-lyric what Chaucer expresses in narrative verse, namely the insight that moments of great human dignity and deep psychological commitment (such as afflict the "true lover") can (and must) coexist with moments of great ridiculousness. Like Chaucer, Dafydd understood how closely nobility and human folly could be aligned, how even a relatively minor shift in perspective can change everything. This, we would argue, is not an insight open to the more sober Dante and Petrarch. It is certainly true that Dafydd shares with the author of the *Commedia* a very sincere apprehension of the sort of power that *love* (or, at times, erotic obsession) can exert upon one's soul, but he more strikingly shares with Chaucer both an earthy sense of humor and a superb sense of irony. Poetry in English would, I think, have to wait for the work of John Donne at the turn of the seventeenth century before it produced a lyric poet so earnest and insightful, and yet also so deeply funny, about the subject of love as the Welshman Dafydd ap Gwilym.

Despite his deep affinity with the great European poets of his day, we should still emphasize that Dafydd's genius is largely homegrown, as surely his range of references suggest. The women of Dafydd's poems, for instance, are not Dante's abstractly named *Beatrice* (= "she who blesses") or Petrarch's *Laura* (after the laurel tree) but drawn from Welsh legend and traditional verse: *Eigr, Tegau, Enid.* Wales itself could surely supply all the feminine beauty the world could need, Dafydd's verse would seem to suggest. And the foremost women in Dafydd's work, Dyddgu and Morfudd, give the impression not of being allegorical, idealized figures but instead of being living, breathing, historical, *Welsh* women, though one can certainly register a difference in his attitudes toward the two that reveals perhaps a deeper contour of his poetic persona. In the poems addressed to the dark-haired and aristocratic

Dyddgu, (such as "The Magpie's Message" in this collection), Dafydd seems more cautious and poetically more conventional, though he does not hesitate to blend continental traditions of love-lyric into his verses for her. With the poems to golden-haired Morfudd, however, we find Dafydd more "himself"—or, at least, more solidly settled in the dramatic persona he most vividly and habitually occupies. Though he of course praises Morfudd's beauty and expresses what appears to be a sincere longing for her, as a piece like "Morfudd's Arms" illustrates, his relationship with Morfudd—whether real or fictional or something in between—affords him the opportunity to strike a number of new poses that had been struck before neither in previous Welsh poetry nor in mainstream European love-lyric. He chides Morfudd and cajoles her; he praises her beauty and then half-retracts his praises; he pines for her and then criticizes her greying hair. All in all, these poses are distinctly anti-Petrarchan, and only Chaucer's most unreliable and specious narrators (like the Pardoner or the Wife of Bath) ever manage to walk such a fine line without descending into either blatant self-contradiction or bathos.

In fact, the wry irony which Dafydd evinces about the state of being in love, and about the state of his beloved, in the Morfudd poems and in many another poem addressed to or written about an unnamed or dimly-named lover (there are Elens, Lyneds and Nyfs waiting in the wings), hearkens back more insistently to the classical Roman Ovid than to any of his medieval near-contemporaries. Ovid is a frequent presence in Dafydd's poetry and is, in fact, one of the few other poets Dafydd ever mentions by name. Though he never quotes the Latin poet directly, Dafydd's verse is, in a sense, awash in Ovid. In "The Fox," the speaker's sylvan hideaway is referred to as "Ovid's leaves"; another poem dubs the thrushcock, as a bird who joyfully announces love, "Ovid's man"; in others still, "Ovid" becomes a direct epithet for the love-poet just as "Ovid's girl" can stand in for the beloved; and so on. One poem even coins the term *ofyddiaeth*, which tellingly seems to mean both "the art of love" (a not-so-oblique reference to the *Ars Amatoria*) and "the craft of poetry" itself.

But if Dafydd asserts himself as a student of Ovid, we might well ask in what such discipleship might consist. On the one hand, as many of Dafydd's references suggest, Ovid might have seemed simply a conventional, go-to authority for writers of love poetry. On the other hand, Dafydd's insights on love would seem to draw more broadly—and more deeply—from the Ovidian well. It's actually difficult to ascertain the exact extent of Dafydd's exposure to Ovid, or even to Roman literature in general. Scholars have identified a few rather definite references to Ovid's *Ars Amatoria*, and they suppose Dafydd to have received some rudimentary training in the Latin language at the old *clas* monastery of Llanbadarn Fawr or at the Cistercian chapter house at Strata Florida. What is clear is that, unlike so many of the other medieval writers influenced by Ovid (who had been in high vogue since the early twelfth century and an especial favorite among medieval university students), Dafydd appears less obviously to treat Ovid's works as a rich manual for erotic behavior, though many of his scurrilous comments do seem "Ovidian" in this sense. He appears instead to have read "through" the mere surface content, articulating a canny perception of Ovid's deeper and more penetrating insights about the nature of love. We might especially align Dafydd's poems with some of the great figures out of Ovid's *Metamorphoses*. Ovid's myth of Daphne, for one, seems almost a master narrative underwriting so many of Dafydd's poems. Fleeing from Apollo, the Roman god of music and poetry, the nymph Daphne manages to remain tantalizingly out of reach as the god pursues her. Just as Apollo catches her, she is wondrously transformed into a laurel tree, and the god, unable to satisfy his desire for the maiden, takes consolation in making out of this new tree's leaves and branches a laurel wreath, which becomes thereafter the crowning symbol of poetic achievement (as Petrarch also knew). The myth expresses, among other things, the idea that art itself is a sort of displacement of unfulfilled desire.

It is this same dynamic that motivates so many of Dafydd's most memorable poems. In "The Mist," again, the meteorological obstacle to the fulfillment of the speaker's romantic plans at least affords the occasion for a poetic diatribe against the mist itself: love unfulfilled. A similar poetic energy obtains in "His Shadow" and "The Magpie's Message" and "The Clock" and even in "The Dream." While the myth of Daphne serves as a steady presence throughout, other myths from Ovid's *Metamorphoses* also haunt Dafydd's poems. There are parallels with the Pyramus and Thisbe story in "The Window," echoes of the Actaeon myth (where hunter and hunted become impossibly conflated) in "The Fox," a strange inversion of the Tereus and Procne story in "The Magpie's Message," and reverberations of the myth of Orpheus everywhere.

In an array of poetic stances almost as varied as Ovid's constantly shifting *Metamorphoses* itself, Dafydd's poems seem keenly aware that every desire transforms both the desirer and the object: all are changed. If, as both T. S. Eliot and Harold Bloom have argued, the true measure of a poet can be gleaned from the earlier writers he chooses as poetic models and rivals, then Dafydd ap Gwilym, a self-confessed "Ovid's man," is in fine company indeed.

In the end, this is Dafydd ap Gwilym's great achievement. In a single gesture, he both invents the medieval Welsh love poem and simultaneously generates its antidote. His poems reveal that he was familiar with the old dance of love but also that he understood all too well an insight that owes as much to Augustine as it does to Ovid: that desire is endless. In what is probably among his last poems—and it is the piece that closes this volume—Dafydd presents a speaker of advanced age musing ruefully on a life vainly spent dallying in love and verse:

> …gone dreams of fame, hope of amours,
> gone all memory of my verses,
> gone all jesting, all desire vanished,
> gone those stories boasting of conquests,
> gone all affection. Unless she beckons.

There, at the threshold, Dafydd—perhaps tongue in cheek, perhaps deadly earnest—invites us back into the house of leaves that are his poems to experience the exhilaration and pain and mockery of love again. And again.

—*Michael Faletra*

Translating Dafydd

The amorous challenges described so amusingly by Dafydd ap Gwilym are not unlike those encountered when translating him. Just as Morfudd and Dyddgu and the other girls who flirt with him, come close to an understanding, and then retreat, so all attempts to match his poems frustrate us by keeping their distance.

The Welsh originals are wonderfully complex, enriched by a battery of metrical and stylistic devises that have few parallels in modern English poetry. The *cywydd*, Dafydd's characteristic form, is a poem of thirty or more lines, in rhyming couplets of seven syllables, where the rhymes are pairs of stressed and unstressed syllables. At the same time, *cywyddau* employ the various forms of *cynghanedd*, in which matched syllables, repeated consonants, or rhymed word-endings chime across the two halves of a line.

Of the purely stylistic devices, *sangiadau* are interruptions in the form of asides, usually occupying a half line; *dyfalu* is the habit of piled-up comparisons, often approaching absurdity; and in *cymeriad* the poet creates long runs of lines with the same initial letter.

Of all the compromises available in matching these intricate patterns, the least profitable is the attempt to reproduce exactly the syllabics, rhyming, and assonance of the *cywydd*. Matching the rhymes of lines as short as seven syllables is unattainable without taking frequent liberties with the sense. It did, however, seem possible to us to make use of *cynghanedd's* patterns of alliteration, assonance, and half rhyme, along with echoes of *sangiad, dyfalu,* and *cymeriad,* to convey something of Dafydd's virtuosity.

It hardly needs saying that his verbal pyrotechnics are a product of this poet's lively and in many ways dissident personality. Translation is a form of necromancy, an attempt to resurrect a writer in another place and at another time. Dafydd used all his verbal resources as spells to call up a fox, a girl, a troublesome mist, so vividly that they still spring to life in our day. We owe it to him to do the same for his poems in English dress. If in our versions the poet seems uninhibited, eccentric, and outrageously ambitious, we will have partly succeeded.

14

We have profited from consulting the excellent versions of Richard Morgan Loomis and Rachel Bromwich, both based on the editorial work of Sir Thomas Parry. We have also enjoyed the lively rhymed translations of Idris and David Bell, and those of Rolfe Humphries. The facing page texts are reproduced with permission from the standard edition *Cerddi Dafydd ap Gwilym* edited by Dafydd Johnston et al., (University of Wales Press, 2010). We have taken two liberties in our use of that text: on one occasion, in the second stanza of "The Rattle Bag," we allowed a reading from Parry to influence our version. And in the matter of stanza division, we have differed from the breaks in *Cerddi*, which are indicated by indents. We have removed those indents, but for ease of comparison have divided the Welsh text to correspond with our stanza breaks.

Earlier versions of some of these translations were published in the online journal of the Iowa International Writing Program, *91st Meridian*, Issue 4.2 (Winter 2006), in the collection *Some Business of Affinity* (Five Seasons Press 2006), and in Mary Szybist's essay "There Interposed a ———: A Few Considerations of Poetic Drama," in *The Writer's Notebook II* (Tin House Books, 2012).

Warm thanks to Christopher Merrill, Natasa Durovicova, Glenn Storhaug, and Mary Szybist.

—Paul Merchant and Michael Faletra

A Note on the Cover Painting

Dafydd ap Gwilym was born in mid Wales and writes with affection about his home territory in Ceredigion, but in his wanderings he was familiar with the north (Gwynedd), especially with the island of Anglesey, and he spent much of his youth in the south (Dyfed). His friend Madog Benfras called him "the nightingale of Dyfed" and another contemporary, Iolo Goch, spoke of him as "the hawk of south Welsh girls." So it is appropriate that the moody landscape painting on our cover is a view from the heart of south Wales, the estuary at Penclawdd, near Swansea.

The painting is by David Bell, son of Sir Harold Idris Bell, the noted British Museum scholar of Welsh literature and of the papyri of Roman Egypt. Father and son were the translators of the charming *Dafydd ap Gwilym, Fifty Poems* of 1942. The painting was a gift to my father from David Bell, his colleague on the Welsh Arts Council. Other paintings by David Bell can be viewed at the Arts UK web site *artuk.org*. I am grateful to the artist's son Dafydd Bell for permission to reproduce this image.

—*Paul Merchant*

Unless She Beckons

Y Cloc

Cynnar fodd, cain arfeddyd,

Canu'dd wyf fi can hawdd fyd

I'r dref wiw ger Rhiw Rheon

Ar gwr y graig, a'r gaer gron.

Yno, gynt ei enw a gad,

Y mae dyn a'm adwaeniad.

Hawddamor heddiw yma

Hyd yn nhyddyn y dyn da.

Beunoeth, foneddigddoeth ferch,

Y mae honno i'm hannerch.

Bryd cwsg ym, a bradw y'i caid,

Breuddwyd yw, braidd y dywaid,

A'm pen ar y gobennydd,

Acw y daw cyn y dydd

Yng ngolwg, eang eilun,

Angel bach yng ngwely bun.

Tybiaswn o'm tyb isod

The Clock

Rising early
   eager to please,
purely, simply
   I sing this praise
for the hilltop refuge,
   handsome Rheon
that crowns its crag
   with a castle circle.
A girl lives there
   long loved for her graces,
a fine-grained girl
   who granted me favors.
Today I come
   to cover with glory
her house, her home
   my honey, my lady,
that gentle girl
   that winsome woman
who slides to my side
   in my midnight slumbers.

This boy falls asleep
   betrayed by exhaustion,
and sees (in a dream,
   that goes without saying,
my heavy head
   propped on the pillow),
who's beside me
   before day's dawning,
glimmering to view
   a gaudy vision:
my ghostly soul
   in my girl's sheets sleeping.
This was my thought,
   that I was with her,

Gan fy mun gynnau fy mod.

Pell oedd rhyngof, cof a'i cais,

A'i hwyneb pan ddihunais.

Och i'r cloc yn ochr y clawdd

Du ei ffriw a'm deffroawdd.

Difwyn fo'i ben a'i dafod

A'i ddwy raff iddo a'i rod,

A'i bwysau, pellennau pŵl,

A'i fuarthau a'i forthwl,

A'i hwyaid yn tybiaid dydd,

A'i felinau aflonydd.

Cloc anfwyn mal clec ynfyd

Cobler brwysg, cabler ei bryd,

Cleddau eurych celwyddawg,

Cnecian ci yn cnocian cawg,

Mynychglap mewn mynachglos

Melin ŵyll yn malu nos.

A fu sadler, crwper crach,

cuddling closely
            as in the old days,
but how far distant
            her darling features
(where, memory?)
            when I awakened.

God damn that clock
            close by the hedge
with its sooty dial
            destroying my slumbers,
its empty head,
            clattering tongue,
its round pulleys
            and purposeless ropes,
its swinging weights
            blunt ball-shapes,
a hellish barnyard
            busy with hammering,
some idiot ducks
            serenading daybreak,
merciless millstones
            grimly grinding.

Cruel clock
            with your crazed clattering,
drunken cobbler
            cursing his destiny,
tinker's chisel
            chipping at entrails,
hellhound's whelp
            gnawing his platter,
warning clapper
            waking the cloister,
ghost windmill
            grinding at midnight.
No saddler scratching

Neu deiler anwadalach?

Oer ddilen ar ei ddolef

Am fy nwyn yma o nef.

Cael ydd oeddwn, coel ddiddos,

Hun o'r nef am hanner nos

Ym mhlygau hir freichiau hon,

Ymhlith Deifr ym mhleth dwyfron.

A welir mwy, alar maeth,

Wlad Eigr, ryw weledigaeth?

Eto rhed ati ar hynt,

Freuddwyd, ni'th ddwg afrwyddynt.

Gofyn i'r dyn dan aur do

A ddaw hun iddi heno

I roi golwg o'r galon,

Nith yr haul, unwaith ar hon.

his scabby crupper,
no rogue roof-tiler
                vied with such vertigo.
To hell with its bell
                its wearisome wail,
keeping me wakeful
                cheated of heaven.

I'd found a shelter
                so snug and secure,
heavenly housing
                for midnight slumbers
held in her slender
                arms' embraces,
full on the breast
                of my famous beauty.
Where again
                (food for anguish)
could I find her like
                in this land of legend?

Run and look now,
                you'll remember,
dream, just take
                the dependable track.
Ask my girl
                with the golden hair
if she'll return
                to sleep this evening,
so I can gaze on her
                (heart of gold,
sunshine's niece)
                just one kind instant.

Merched Llanbadarn

Plygu rhag llid yr ydwyf,
Pla ar holl ferched y plwyf!
Am na chefais, drais drawsoed,
Ohonun yr un erioed,
Na morwyn, fwyn ofynaig,
Na merch fach na gwrach na gwraig.

Pa rusiant, pa ddireidi,
Pa fethiant na fynnant fi?
Pa ddrwg i riain feinael
Yng nghoed tywylltew fy nghael?
Nid oedd gywilydd iddi
Yng ngwâl dail fy ngweled i.

Ni bu amser na charwn —
Ni bu mor lud hud â hwn —
Anad gwŷr annwyd Garwy,
Yn y dydd ai un ai dwy,
Ac er hynny nid oedd nes
Ym gael un no'm gelynes.

Ni bu Sul yn Llanbadarn
Na bewn, ac eraill a'i barn,
A'm wyneb at y ferch goeth
A'm gwegil at Dduw gwiwgoeth.
A chwedy'r hir edrychwyf
Dros fy mhlu ar draws fy mhlwyf,

Syganai y fun befrgroyw
Wrth y llall hylwyddgall, hoyw:
'Godinabus fydd golwg —
Gŵyr ei ddrem gelu ei ddrwg —
Y mab llwyd wyneb mursen
A gwallt ei chwaer ar ei ben.'

'Ai'n rhith hynny yw ganthaw?'
Yw gair y llall geir ei llaw,

The Girls of Llanbadarn

Frustration, my old friend, pronounce
a plague on all Llanbadarn's girls.
I've paid the whole pack deep devotion
without reward, not a single smile,
from tender virgin (test of virtue)
young hussy, hag, or wanton wife.

Did I ever hesitate, once hold back?
What slight could rate such weight of scorn?
Would she lose out, that dark-eyed lass,
to seek me deep in the forest's center?
What shame to dare that shaded den,
loving me there in my lair of leaves?

I dedicate from dawn till evening
to chants of love, loosing my charms
of primitive ancestral potency.
Each day I woo a dame or two.
My cruel lovers prove so gentle
they greet me like an enemy.

Each Sunday in Llanbadarn church
(judge if you will) I risk my soul,
turning my face to those fine tempters
and the nape of my neck to God's altar,
hidden behind my hat's brave feather,
perusing the pews with lingering lust.

Then a lively maiden whispers low
to her winsome quick companion:
"See over there that whey-faced flirt
wearing his hair in curls like a girl?
I'd never risk such a roving lover,
that mischief-maker, scholar of sin."

"You'd expect no better from this boy,"
murmurs the other behind her hand.

'Ateb nis caiff tra fo byd,
Wtied i ddiawl, beth ynfyd!'
Talmithr ym rheg y loywferch,
Tâl bychan am syfrdan serch.

Rhaid oedd ym fedru peidiaw
Â'r foes hon, breuddwydion braw.
Gorau ym fyned fal gŵr
Yn feudwy, swydd anfadwr.
O dra disgwyl, dysgiad certh,
Drach 'y nghefn, drych anghyfnerth,

Neur dderyw ym, gerddrym gâr,
Bengamu heb un gymar.

"He'll angle a lifetime for his answer.
Let him go hang, he's a giddy thing."
A raw reward from that lovely lady,
for wild wooing a paltry payment.

Must I say farewell to fair ones,
bidding adieu to all my dreams?
An outlaw lodged in a hermit's cell,
in a shady haven I'll hide my shame.
My lesson learned, my love days done,
I'll bury for good my backward glances.

I followed musicians, merry fellows,
now I live solitary, sleep alone.

Ei Gysgod

Doe'r oeddwn dan oreuddail
Yn aros gwen, Elen ail,
Yn gochel glaw dan gochl glas
Y fedwen fal ynfydwas.
Ucho gwelwn ryw eulun
Yn sefyll yn hyll ei hun.
Ysgodigaw draw ar draws
Ohonof fal gŵr hynaws
A chroesi rhag echrysaint
Y corff mau â swynau saint.

'Dywed, a phaid â'th dewi,
Yma, wyt ŵr, pwy wyd ti'.
'Myfi, a gad dy ymofyn,
Dy gysgod hynod dy hun.
Taw, er Mair, na lestair les,
Ym fynegi fy neges.
Dyfod ydd wyf, defod dda,
I'th ymyl o'm noeth yma
I ddangos, em addwyngŵyn,
Rhyw beth wyd. Mae rhaib i'th ddwyn'.

'Nage, ŵr hael, anwr hyll,
Nid wyf felly, dwf ellyll.
Godrum gafr o'r un gyfrith,
Tebygach wyd, tebyg chwith,
I drychiolaeth hiraethlawn
Nog i ddyn mewn agwedd iawn.
Heusor mewn secr yn cecru,
Llorpau gwrach ar dudfach du;
Bugail ellyllon bawgoel,
Bwbach ar lun manach moel;

Grëwr yn chwarae griors,
Grŷr llawn yn pori cawn cors;
Garan yn bwrw ei gwryd,

28

His Shadow

Dafydd: As I lurked among green-glint leaves,
                 lying in wait for my lily-white girl
(Helen's equal) under birch boughs,
                 rain refuge for a lovelorn lad,
yesterday rose a rude apparition
                 sliding next to me, a vexing sight.
I skipped aslant, avoiding its touch,
                 and, genteel gentleman that I am,
armed my glance against mischance
                 blessing my body with Christ's cross.

Speak, I stammered, no secrets here,
                 what manner of man is met with me?
Shadow: See, and make no mystery,
                 I am simply your own self's shadow.
Now hush, by our Lady, let me alone
                 to bear as burden this tale I tell.
I have come, on my best behavior,
                 wearing my true dress, nakedness,
to judge and say (that jeweled array)
                 what spell, what magic makes up you.

Dafydd: No, I'm merely a man, you monster,
                 not to be entrapped as a troll.
But you, you bloated sway-backed goat,
                 you shape-shifter, mirror-glimmerer,
ghost belonging in a world of longing,
                 never a man with a brave demeanor,
you're a shepherd cheating at checkers,
                 a witch stalking on swarthy thighs,
engrosser of goblins mired in mud,
                 a bald bugbear with a priest's pate.

A rider astride a hobby-horse,
                 a heron feeding on wetland reeds,
a crane with spread wings, ready to fly,

Garrau'r ŵyll, ar gwr yr ŷd;
Wyneb palmer o hurthgen,
Brawd du o ŵr mewn brat hen;
Drum corff wedi'i droi mewn carth,
Ble buost, hen bawl buarth?'
'Llawer dydd, yt pes lliwiwn,
Gyda thi. Gwae di o'th wn!'

'Pa anaf arnaf amgen
A wyddost ti, wddw ystên,
Ond a ŵyr pob synhwyrawl
O'r byd oll? Yty baw diawl!
Ni chatcenais fy nghwmwd,
Ni leddais, gwn, leddf ysgwd;
Ni theflais ieir â thafl fain,
Ni fwbechais rai bychain;
Nid af yn erbyn fy nawn,
Ni rwystrais wraig gŵr estrawn'.

'Myn fy nghred, pe mynegwn
I'r rhai ni ŵyr 'r hyn a wn,
Dir ennyd cyn torri annog,
Fy nghred, y byddud ynghrog'.

'Ymogel, tau, y magl tost,
Rhag addef 'rhawg a wyddost
Mwy no phe bai tra fai'n fau
Gowni ar gwr y genau'.

an army of owls at the field's edge.
You sport the smirk of a stunned pilgrim,
                    a moody monk in a ragged habit,
a body bound for a hempen shroud,
                    a slant stick stuck in the muck.
Shadow: But all day long I'll be your bane,
                    marking you with my keen eye.

Dafydd: What can you say to wound me now,
                    you churlish lout with a pitcher's spout?
Every wise fellow knows my faults
                    through the wide world. By the devil's dung
I never jest on my native nest,
                    never flashed knife to flush a life,
never chucked stones to scare the chicks,
                    nor made ghost-grimaces, frightening fellows.
I'm ready to share my skills so well
                    my neighbor's wife won't speak to my shame.

Shadow: My god, but I could tell such tales,
                    recite the rosary of your various villainies,
in minutes you'd be manacled
                    and snatched away to stretch your neck.

Dafydd: Stop there! Don't set that snare for me.
                    I warn you, warble a single word
of my so-called sins, I'll sew your mouth
                    with the same stitch stops a corpse's lips.

Y Breuddwyd

Fal yr oeddwn, gwn heb gêl,
Yn dargwsg mewn lle dirgel,
Gwelais ar glais dichlais dydd
Breuddwyd ar ael boreuddydd.

Tybiwn fy mod yn rhodiaw
A llu bytheiaid i'm llaw,
Ac yn cerdded y gwledydd
A'r tir adwaenwn hyd dydd,
Ac i fforest yn gestwng,
Teg blas, nid tŷ taeog blwng.
Gollyngwn i yn ddioed,
Debygwn, y cŵn i'r coed.
Cynydd da, iawn ddawn ddifri,
Ar a dybiwn oeddwn i.
Clywwn oriau, lleisiau llid,
Canu'n aml, cŵn yn ymlid.
Ewig wen goruwch llennyrch
A welwn, carwn y cyrch,
A rhawd fytheiaid ar hynt
Yn ei hôl, iawn eu helynt.
Cyrchu'r allt yn ddiwalltrum
A thros ddwy esgair a thrum,
A thrachefn dros y cefnydd
Ar hynt un helynt â hydd,
A dyfod wedy'i dofi,
A minnau'n ddig, i'm nawdd i.
Dwyffroen noeth—deffroi wneuthum.
Ŵr glwth, yn y bwth y bûm.

Cyrchais gongl ar ddehonglydd
Drannoeth fal y doeth y dydd.

The Dream

Once upon a time
I was taking a nap
I happened to see
a dream on the brow

(there's a den I know)
in that secret place
at dawn's first glow
of day's fresh face.

I saw myself
with a pack of hounds
Deep in the woods
not at all the hovel
I loosed the hounds
as I imagined
In angry voices
the mingled song
A handy hunter
just then I glimpsed
a milk-white doe
with my pack of hounds
tracking her down
She took to the slope
crossed two ridges
doubled back
the very course
In the end she came
under my thrall
My nostrils flared,
faint with hunger,

alone and strolling
held close enough.
I found a fine dwelling
of some dull oaf.
into a clearing
without a thought.
the dogs were baying,
of hounds in pursuit.
in my own opinion,
far off in the fields
(how I love the chase)
hot on her heels,
on her very course.
the whole hill's breast,
on the horizon,
over the crest
a stag had just taken.
tamed at last
(my heart was swelling).
I awakened fast,
inside the dwelling.

When day was dawning
I found an old woman

greedy for meaning,
I could trust.

Cefais hynafgwraig gyfiawn
Pan oedd ddydd yn ddedwydd iawn.
Addef a wneuthum iddi,
Goel nos, fal y gwelwn i.
'Rho Duw, wraig gall, pe gallud
Rhyw derfyn ar hyn o hud,
Ni chyfflybwn, gwn ganclwyf,
Neb â thi. Anobaith wyf'.

'Da beth, y diobeithiwr,
Yw dy freuddwyd, od wyd ŵr:
Y cŵn heb gêl a welud
I'th law, pe gwypud iaith lud,
Dy hwylwyr, diau helynt,
Dy lateion eon ŷnt,
A'r ewig wen unbennes
A garud ti, hoen geirw tes.

Diau yw hyn y daw hi
I'th nawdd, a Duw i'th noddi'.

At earliest daylight
I came to her
the night's message
"By heaven, wise woman,
to unriddle this spell,
you'd cure me of
with your rare skill.

downright eagerly
and freely confessed
as it seemed to me.
if you know
O, if you can
a hundred blows
I'm a hopeless case."

"To be without hope
I'll tell you your dream
The dogs (it's clear)
tight in your hand
those clever hunters
are your ambassadors
And the white doe
so hot she shimmers

is a good beginning.
if you're a true man.
that you were holding
(words stick in the mind)
coursing freely
ready to rove.
that is your lady
a rippling wave.

And I'll say more:
under your thrall

she'll come to you
if God stays true."

Y Rhugl Groen

Fal yr oeddwn, fawl rwyddaf,

Y rhyw ddiwrnod o'r haf

Dan wŷdd rhwng mynydd a maes

Yn gorllwyn fy nyn geirllaes,

Dyfod a wnaeth, nid gwaeth gwad,

Lle'r eddewis, lloer ddiwad.

Cydeiste, cywiw destun,

Amau o beth, mi a bun;

Cyd-draethu, cyn henu hawl,

Geiriau â bun ragorawl.

A ni felly, any oedd,

Yn deall serch ein deuoedd,

Dyfod a wnaeth, noethfaeth nych,

Dan gri, rhyw feistri fystrych,

Salw ferw fach, sain gwtsach sail,

O begor yn rhith bugail.

The Rattle Bag

As I reclined
        (a reason for praise)
one summer noontime
        under the trees,
in between
        mountain and moor
waiting for
        my girl to appear,
that soft speaker
        turned up true
a reliable moon
        rising on cue.
We sat together
        began to debate
what boys
        with girls negotiate,
exchanging
        in the time available
phrases my fine girl
        found agreeable.

How shy she was!
        We talked, drank mead
one hour's dalliance,
        heaven indeed.
When a sudden sound
        a mannerless madness
assaulted our senses
        a scurvy sadness,
the shrill speech
        of a sack of lies,
a grim goblin
        in a shepherd's guise,

A chanto'r oedd, cyhoedd cas,

Rugl groen flin gerngrin gorngras.

Canodd, felengest westfach,

Y rhugl groen; och i'r hegl grach!

Ac yno heb ddigoni

Gwiw fun a wylltiodd, gwae fi!

Pan glybu hon, fron fraenglwy,

Nithio'r main, ni thariai mwy.

Dan Grist, ni bu dôn o Gred,

Cynar enw, cyn erwined:

Cod ar ben ffon yn sonio,

Cloch sain o grynfain a gro;

Crwth cerrig Seisnig yn sôn

Crynedig mewn croen eidion;

Cawell teirmil o chwilod,

Callor dygyfor, du god;

Cadwades gwaun, cydoes gwellt,

who held in his hand
                    like an enemy flag
a four-cornered, floppy
                    rude rattle-bag.

It was beating time
                    on his flabby flank
this bag of stones
                    on that scabby shank.
We were close to the boil
                    my consort and I,
but my darling paled,
                    her passion died.
Her faint heart failed
                    at the stones' sharp sound.
Too shy she'd grown
                    to stand her ground.
And, Christ, no clatter
                    in Christendom
no matter its name
                    could match the thrum
of that harsh pebble-bag
                    hung from its pole,
that bawling bell
                    of grit and gravel.

Those Saxon stones
                    a fiddle ill-played,
pebbles shaken
                    in a bullock's hide,
a crabbed cage filled
                    with three thousand insects,
a seething cauldron,
                    a sackful of nuts,
a mower of meadows
                    as old as grass-clippings,

Groenddu feichiog o grinddellt.

Cas ei hacen gan heniwrch,

Cloch ddiawl, a phawl yn ei ffwrch.

Greithgrest garegddwyn grothgro,

Yn gareiau byclau y bo.

Oerfel i'r carl gwasgarlun,

Amên, a wylltiodd fy mun.

a dark leather bag
                  burdened with shavings,
a scourge to scare
                  an ancient hind,
a bell from hell
                  with a pole in its groin,
a leather belly
                  (filled with stone pieces)
to be sliced lengthwise
                  into shoe-laces.

May he be shivered
                  to shreds, that churl
(amen to that prayer!)
                  who panicked my girl.

Yr Wylan

Yr wylan deg ar lanw, dioer,
Unlliw ag eiry neu wenlloer,
Dilwch yw dy degwch di,
Darn fal haul, dyrnfol heli.
Ysgafn ar don eigion wyd,
Esgudfalch edn bysgodfwyd.
Yngo'r aud wrth yr angor
Lawlaw â mi, lili môr.
Llythr unwaith lle'th ariannwyd,
Lleian ym mrig llanw môr wyd.

Cyweirglod bun, cai'r glod bell,
Cyrch ystum caer a chastell.
Edrych a welych, wylan,
Eigr o liw ar y gaer lân.
Dywaid fy ngeiriau dyun,
Dewised fi, dos hyd fun.
Byddai'i hun, beiddia'i hannerch,
Bydd fedrus wrth fwythus ferch
Er budd; dywaid na byddaf,
Fwynwas coeth, fyw onis caf.

Ei charu'r wyf, gwbl nwyf nawdd,
Och wŷr, erioed ni charawdd
Na Merddin wenithfin iach,
Na Thaliesin ei thlysach.
Siprys dyn giprys dan gopr,
Rhagorbryd rhy gyweirbropr.

Och wylan, o chai weled
Grudd y ddyn lanaf o Gred,
Oni chaf fwynaf annerch,
Fy nihenydd fydd y ferch.

Seagull

White gull (my God!) above waves,
the color of snow, of silver moon,
bearer of beauty without a blemish,
sun's gleam, gauntlet of sea-spray.
Weightless, drifting over deep waters,
so fleet and haughty, fine fish-forager,
agile in air, anchored to oceans,
we touch fingers, wave-foam lily,
shining sheet silver with script,
pure as a nun in her salt cell.

The girl I sing, her fame will spread
far about, to castle and keep.
Sharp-eyed gull, swoop to see
a maid in her eyrie, another Igraine.
Speak this single phrase of friendship:
let her love Dafydd. Go to the girl,
if you see her alone, dare to greet her.
Use all your wit, for she's a wise one,
to win her over. Say these words:
this captive lad can't live without her.

I love her, I make no bones about it.
No man ever desired so deeply.
I think neither Merlin, the honey-tongued,
nor true Taliesin wooed dearer damsel.
This tall girl's curls are spun copper,
such grace she has, in such sweet guise.

Ah gull, when you come to contemplate
the prettiest cheek in Christendom,
unless she send me a tender message,
this girl will earn me an early grave.

Offeren y Llwyn

Lle digrif y bûm heddiw
Dan fentyll y gwyrddgyll gwiw,
Yn gwarando ddechrau dydd

Y ceiliog bronfraith celfydd
Yn canu ynglyn alathr,
Arwyddion a llithion llathr.

Pellennig, Pwyll ei annwyd,
Pell siwrneiai'r llatai llwyd.
Yma doeth o swydd goeth Gaer

Am ei erchi o'm eurchwaer,
Geiriog, hyd pan geir gwarant,
Sef y cyrch, yn entyrch nant.

Amdano yr oedd gamsai
O flodau mwyn geinciau Mai,
A'i gasul, dybygesynt,

O esgyll, gwyrdd fentyll, gwynt.
Nid oedd yna, myn Duw mawr,
Ond aur oll yn do'r allawr.

Morfudd a'i hanfonasai
Mydr ganiadaeth mab maeth Mai.
Mi a glywwn mewn gloywiaith

Ddatganu, nid methu, maith,
Ddarllain i'r plwyf, nid rhwyf rhus,
Efengyl yn ddifyngus.

Codi ar fryn ynn yna
Afrlladen o ddeilien dda,
Ac eos gain fain fangaw

Forest Communion

Pure morning joy
under leafy canopy
at wake of day I heard

> the clever cock thrush
> pour his glittering song
> melts the stoniest heart.

Sober-accented
foreign love-message
from as far as Carmarthen

> sent by my gold girl
> sung across borders
> straight to this valley.

He wore a chasuble
speckled with may-blossom
fit for a celebrant

> his surplice the wind
> and on the altar
> the gleam of gold.

Singer of canticles
pouring the gospel
into eager ears,

> Morfudd sent him
> this clever chorister
> May's foster child.

A leaf was raised
as consecrate host
while the slender nightingale

O gwr y llwyn ger ei llaw,
Clerwraig nant, i gant a gân
Cloch aberth, clau a chwiban,

A dyrchafael yr aberth
Hyd y nen uwchben y berth,
A chrefydd i'n Dofydd Dad

Â charegl nwyf a chariad.
Bodlon wyf i'r ganiadaeth,
Bedwlwyn o'r coed mwyn a'i maeth.

in a nearby copse
our valley poet
trilled the sanctus bell

Celebrating
in sight of God
our hedge-communion

I drained the loving-cup
relished that song
and its green birthplace.

Y Ffenestr

Cerddais o fewn cadleisiau,
Cerdd wamal fu'r mwngial mau,
Gan ystlys, dyrys diroedd,
Hundy bun, hyn o dyb oedd.
Da arganfod, dewr geinferch,
Drwy frig y llwyn er mwyn merch,
Ffyrf gariad, dygiad agerw,
Ffenestr gadarn ar ddarn dderw.
Erchais gusan, gwedd lanach,
I'r fun drwy'r dderw ffenestr fach,

Gem addwyn, oedd gam iddi,
Gomeddodd, ni fynnodd fi;
Astrus fu'r ffenestr oestraul,
Lle'i rhoed i ddwyn lleufer haul.
Ni bwy' hen o bu o hud
Ffenestr â hon un ffunud,

Dieithr hwyl, dau uthr helynt,
Yr hon ar Gaerlleon gynt
Y dôi Felwas o draserch
Drwyddi heb arswydi serch,
Cur tremynt cariad tramawr,
Gynt ger tŷ ferch Gogfran Gawr.

Cyd cawn fod pan fai'n odi
Hwyl am y ffenestr â hi,
Ni chefais elw fal Melwas,
Nychu'r grudd, Dduw, nacha'r gras.

Betem, fi a'm dlifem dlos,
Wyneb yn wyneb nawnos,
Heb ŵyl sâl, heb olau sêr,
Heb elw rhwng y ddau biler,
Mwy'r cawdd o boptu'r mur calch,
Finfin, fi a'm dyn feinfalch,

The Window

Wandering my way through a maze of walls
wondering which fickle measures to mumble,
I was lost at first, then came to my senses
under her chamber, just as I'd chosen.
I succeeded in seeing her (my bold beauty).
From behind a bush I viewed my vanquisher
(love grabs us all with a grip of iron)
through a stout window of solid wood.
I begged a kiss (such a lovely face)
from the one behind the small oak window.

Splendid jewel, this time she was cruel,
turned me aside, said she'd not see me.
It stood in my way, that worn window
placed right there as a source of sunlight.
May I never look at another just like it,
a window crossed with a witch's curse.

A man and a woman, reckless romancers,
lived in Caerleon. Love-crazed Melwas
climbed through a window to claim Guinevere.
(There's no desire without dejection;
love without pain's a puny passion.)
She was giant Gogfran's darling daughter.

I was outside (it had started to snow
by her good grace) beyond that window.
I had no reward like Melwas that night.
Her cheek (sweet gift) was kept unkissed.

If only I and my well-set pearl
could spend face to face a nine-day spell,
or one short night, dark with no starlight,
without reward even, inside the woodwork.
I roamed enraged, the limed wall my limit.
There was no lip-lipping my lissom beauty,

Ni allem, eurem wryd,
Gael y ddau ylfin i gyd.
Ni eill dau enau unoed
Drwy ffenestr gyfyngrestr goed,
F'angau graen, fy nghaeu o gred,
'Fengyl rhag ei chyfynged.

Ni phoened neb wrth ffenestr
Rhwng ffanugl nos a rhos restr,
Heb huno, fal y'm poenwyd,
Heb hwyl hoyw am ddyn loyw lwyd.
Torrid diawl, ffenestrawl ffau,
Â phŵl arf ei philerau,
Awchlwyr llid, a'i chlawr llydan,
A'i chlo a'i hallwedd achlân,
Ac a wnaeth, rheolaeth rhus,
Rhyw restr bilerau rhwystrus;

Lladd cannaid a'm lludd cynnif,
A'r llaw a'i lladdodd â llif,
Lladd dihir a'm lludd dyun,
Lluddiodd fi lle 'dd oedd y fun.

no means for me and my gold-set gemstone
to link our beaks in a lusty peck,
to join our jaws, just for an instant
through slim slats, the wood of that window.
(It's the worst of deaths, to die unshriven,
no kiss of peace, in such a close prison.)

No one has suffered so outside a window
between fennel bed and red rose hedge
as I, sleepless, cheated of joy,
longing all night for my loyal lady.
May the devil destroy this den of a window,
fracture its frame with a blunt bludgeon
(force of my fury), smash sturdy shutters,
unlatch both lock and key completely,
along with the man (handcrafter of hindrances)
who raised this rude row of posts and pillars.

Death to the dawn that prevented my purpose,
hammer that hand so smart with a saw-cut,
and batter the lout who lingered between us.
The girl was there, but I never got anywhere.

Y Niwl

Doe Ddifiau, dydd i yfed,
Da fu'm gael, dyfu ym ged,
Coel fawrddysg, cul wyf erddi,
Cyfa serch, y cefais i
Gwrs glwysgainc goris glasgoed
Gyda merch, gadai ym oed.

Nid oedd, o dan hoywDduw Dad,
Dawn iddi, dyn a wyddiad,
Or dôi Difiau, dechrau dydd,
Lawned fûm o lawenydd
Yn myned, gweled gwiwlun,
I'r tir yr oedd feinir fun,

Pan ddoeth yn wir ar hirros
Niwl yn gynhebig i nos.
Rhol fawr a fu'n glawr i'r glaw,
Rhestri gleision i'm rhwystraw,
Rhidyll ystaen yn rhydu,
Rhwyd adar y ddaear ddu,

Cae anghlaer mewn cyfynglwybr,
Carthen anniben yn wybr,
Cwfl llwyd yn cyfliwio llawr,
Cwfert ar bob cwm ceufawr,
Clwydau uchel a welir,
Clais mawr uwch garth, tarth y tir,

Cnu tewlwyd gwynllwyd gwanllaes,
Cyfliw â mwg, cwfl y maes,
Coetgae glaw er lluddiaw lles,
Codarmur cawad ormes,
Twyllai wŷr, tywyll o wedd,
Toron gwrddonig tiredd,

The Mist

Yesterday (Thursday, my drinking day)
was a time for gifts, and turned out well.
It was an omen. Worn to a simple shred
with lust, I received a kind invitation
to a love-tryst in the green cathedral,
a meeting made at my girl's choosing.

No man alive, under God's glory,
knew of my pact with the shapely girl.
At sun's rising that Thursday morning
I leapt from bed brim full of laughter
and set my course to the country spot
where the slim one was expecting me.

But now across the empty moor
a mist came creeping, black as night,
rain's manuscript, a lid clapped on,
gray slanting torrents to snag me,
a tin colander rusting through,
a fowling net on the swarthy soil.

A dark gate blocking a narrow path,
a winnowing sieve tossed up carelessly,
a monk's gray cowl shading the land,
to darken every vale and hollow,
a thorn fence striding the sky, a mighty
bruise on the land, fog on the mountain.

It was like wool, a thin veil of fleece
the color of smoke, a cowl for the field,
a boundary hedge barring my progress,
a coat of armor, a storm to soak me,
a man-deceiver, a face-darkener,
a coarse cloak of country cloth.

Tyrau uchel eu helynt
Tylwyth Gwyn, talaith y gwynt,
Tir a gudd ei ddeurudd ddygn,
Torsed yn cuddio teirsygn,
Tywyllwg, un tew allardd,
Delli byd i dwyllo bardd,

Llydanwe gombr gosombraff,
Ar lled y'i rhodded fal rhaff,
Gwe adrgop, Ffrengigsiop ffrwyth,
Gwan dalar Gwyn a'i dylwyth,
Mwg brych yn fynych a fydd,
Mogodarth cylch meigoedydd,

Anadl arth lle cyfarth cŵn,
Ennaint gwrachïod Annwn,
Gochwith megis gwlith y gwlych,
Habrsiwn tir anehwybrsych.
Haws cerdded nos ar rosydd
I daith nog ar niwl y dydd.

Y sêr a ddaw o'r awyr
Fal fflamau canhwyllau cwyr,
Ac ni ddaw, poen addaw, pŵl
Lloer na sêr Nêr ar nïwl.
Gwladaidd y gwnaeth yn gaethddu
Y niwl fyth, anolau fu.

Lluddiodd ym lwybr dan wybren,
Llatai a ludd llwytu len,
A lluddias ym, gyflym gael,
Myned at fy nyn meinael.

It was a castle right in my path,
hall of the fairy king, wind's territory,
shaggy cheeks shrouding the earth,
torches vying with three last stars
in deep, dense, unseemly darkness,
the world's blinkers, blinding a bard.

A length of expensive cambric
thrown across heavens, a halter
of spidery gossamer, French fabric
over the moorland, fairies' realm,
a thick swath of piebald smoke,
forest mist on a May morning.

A bear's breath, a barking kennel,
ointment smeared on Hell's witches,
sodden dew become oddly sinister,
a discarded suit of damp chain-mail.
I'd sooner walk the pitch-dark heath
than navigate this mist at noon.

Midnight stars brighten the sky,
just like the lights of waxen tapers,
but this morning (bitter memory)
no moon, no stars from God, just mist,
a dark door slammed shut behind me,
fog forever, utter unlight.

Thus was my path curdled by clouds,
a sheet stranding an amorous embassage.
Time flew, and I failed to touch her,
eager for my girl's elegant glances.

Cusan

Hawddamawr, ddeulawr ddilyth,
Haeddai fawl, i heddiw fyth,
Yn rhagorol, dwyol daith,
Rhag doe neu echdoe nychdaith.
Nid oedd debig, Ffrengig ffriw,
Dyhuddiant doe i heddiw.
Nid un wawd, neud anwadal,
Heddiw â doe, hoywdda dâl.
Ie, Dduw Dad, a ddaw dydd
Unlliw â heddiw hoywddydd?
Heddiw y cefais hoywddawn,
Her i ddoe, hwyr yw ei ddawn.

     Cefais werth, gwnaeth ym chwerthin,
     Canswllt a morc, cwnsallt min.
     Cusan fu ym (cyson wyf fi)
     Cain Luned, can oleuni.
     Celennig lerw ddierwin,
     Clyw, er Mair, clo ar y min.
     Ceidw ynof serch y ferch fad,
     Coel mawr gur, cwlm ar gariad.

     Cof a ddaw ynof i'w ddwyn,
     Ciried mawr, cariad morwyn.
     Coron am ganon genau,
     Caerfyrddin cylch y min mau.
     Cain bacs min diorwacserch,
     Cwlm hardd rhwng meinfardd a merch.
     Cynneddf hwn neb niw cennyw,
     Cynnadl dau anadl, da yw.

     Cefais, ac wi o'r cyfoeth,
     Corodyn min dyn mwyn, doeth.
     Cryf wyf o'i gael yn ael nod,
     Crair min disglair mwyn dwysglod.
     Criaf ei wawd, ddidlawd ddadl,

A Kiss

O twice-lucky day, to last longest in memory,
Today of all days rating remembrance,
Gift greater by far than a pilgrim's pathway,
Than the well-worn path I trod just yesterday,
For time past bears foreign features,
No comparison with now's passion.
Yesterday's rhymes were rude rhythms
Beside today's rich rhapsody.
By God the Father, I'd be glad to find
A second such gift, a grant of sweetness.
Today I was traded a lasting lip-token,
A rebuke to yesterday, a tardy gift.

    Came full value, something to smile at,
    Clear five pounds worth, a lip lodgement,
    Constancy's legacy, mouth-memory,
    Clever Lyned's, that glow of lamplight,
    Clean and youthful at the year's closing.
    Credit this, by Mary, it was a lip lock,
    Clasp to the casket of my girl's graces,
    Carrier of love-longing, knotting up knowledge.

    Credit memory, making me constant,
    Claiming my soul, her kindly solace.
    Crown of constraint, rule of reticence,
    Carmarthen's code leading my lips,
    Cool kiss of peace, concealing passion,
    Created a love-knot, a lasting contract.
    Catch us if you can, garrulous gossips,
    Call it the beauty of breath co-mingled.

    Clasping our destiny we drank greedily
    Coming together, coining lip-treasure.
    Courage came from her eyes' enticement,
    Creeping upon me her lush lips' lure,
    Cause of rejoicing, a rich colloquy,

Crynais gan y croyw anadl.
Cwlm cariad mewn tabliad dwbl,
Cwmpasgaer min campusgwbl.

Cyd cefais, ddidrais ddwydrin,
Heiniar mawl, hwn ar 'y min,
Trysor ym yw, trisawr mêl,
Teiroch ym os caiff Turel,
Ac os caiff hefyd, bryd brau,
Mursen fyth, mawrson fwythau.
Ni bu ddrwg, ei gwg a gaf,
Lai no dwrn Luned arnaf.

Inseiliodd a haeddodd hi,
Mul oeddwn, fy mawl iddi.
Ni ddaw o'm tafawd wawdair
Mwy er merch, berw serch a bair,
Eithr a ddêl, uthrwedd wylan,
Ar fy nghred, i Luned lân.

Eiddun anadl cariadloes,
A Dduw, mwy a ddaw i'm oes
Y rhyw ddydd, heulwenddydd wiw,
Am hoywddyn, ym â heddiw?

Created such quivering I spoke quavering,
Close embraced, two clasps enlacing,
Castle guarding her closed lips' garden.

Our two selves twinned, no sign of struggle,
Glimmer of glory, our lips linking.
O triple treasure, a hive of honey,
Triple regret if Tyrrell should get it
(He has his darling, a bold baggage,
A brittle beauty, famed for flirtation)
I'd mourn the loss of my Lyned's lips
More than her frown, her fist at my forehead.

I made her a promise, sealing a pact
(Ass that I was) to sing of her solely,
No word of praise, no poem for a woman
To trip off my tongue (and yet love lingers)
But only for Lyned, the lovely lass
(A solemn promise) would I sing praises.

Love is a breath laden with longing.
O God, will I live to be granted again
A day like today, splendid with sunlight,
Made glad by my girl, a day like today?

Trydydd Cywydd Ymryson
Dafydd ap Gwilym

Gruffudd Gryg, ddirmyg ddarmerth,
Grugiar y gerdd, somgar serth,
Mefl ar dy farf yn Arfon,
Ac ar dy wefl mefl ym Môn.
Doeth wyd, da fu Duw â thi,
Dan nyddu gwddf, dy noddi.
Dianc rhag clêr yn eres
Ydd wyd, taw lysfwyd di-les.

Rhyw elyn beirdd, rhy olud,
Rhywola dy draha drud.
Ffraeth arfaeth, erfain haerllug,
Ffrwyna, diffygia dy ffug.
Gwahawdd nawdd, nyddig fuost,
Gwahardd, du fastardd, dy fost.
Gwae di na elly'n hy hyn,
Gwadu'r cwpl, gwe adrcopyn,

Am ddeugyw, amau ddigawn,
Eryr a iâr, oerwr iawn.
Gair o gamryfyg erwyr,
Garw dy gerdd, y gŵr du gŵyr.
Diwyl dy hwyl i hoywlys,
Dielw ddyn, dy alw ydd ŷs
Draenen gwawd, druenyn gwedd,
Neu eithinen iaith Wynedd.

A chadw cam, o chydcemir
Â thi ar fordwy a thir,
Daith draws, ni wnei dithau draw
Amgenach nag ymgeiniaw.
Hy fydd pawb, dan hoywfodd perth,
Yn absen, ofn wynebserth.
Trafferth flin yw yt, Ruffudd,
Chwyrn braw, od â'r chwarae'n brudd.

Dafydd's Third Assault on Griffith Gryg

Griffith Gryg, first at fault-finding,
prince of the gross and grudging poem,
shame on you, unshaven in Arvon,
shame on you, angry in Anglesey.
In tenderer times, God was your guardian,
and I wove verses primed to protect you,
but you fell foul of the minstrel fraternity,
grew greedy, proved a prey to parasites.

Now you take pride in poet-tormenting,
it's time we tamed your artful arrogance.
You're quick and clever, ready with repartee,
but we'll bridle your tongue, that bold truth-twister.
You headstrong poet, find a place to be hidden,
you can drop your boasting, you dismal bastard.
You're a failed verse-weaver, spinner of spider-webs,
you should be ashamed your skill's escaped you.

You made an odd verse on that brace of birds,
the eagle and hen, perversest of poems
made by a man most reckless in rhyming,
a dismal grouser's dimwitted grumblings.
You waited on great ones, a grand ambition
for a worthless wretch, known for your nonsense,
your thorn songs of a threadbare singer,
rank as gorse in the rough words of Gwynedd.

And any fellow who follows you home
will challenge and chill you with his skill,
on sea or land a sad loss to live with,
leaving you cursing your luck's conclusion.
We're all kings in our cosy thickets,
but in foreign parts all poets are fearful.
I don't respect you. Hearing your verses,
the low outpourings of a loud-mouthed poet,

Cystal wyf, cas dilewfoes,
I'th wlad di â thi i'th oes;

Gwell na thi, gwall a'th ddyun,
Glud fy hawl, i'm gwlad fy hun.
Af i Wynedd, amlwledd ym,
Ar dy dor, ŵr du dirym.
Os cadarn dy farn arnaf,
Main ac aur ym Môn a gaf.
Tithau, o'r lle'th amheuir
O doi di i'r Deau dir,
Ti fydd, cytbar fâr y farn,
Broch yng nghod, braich anghadarn.

Lle clywyf, heb loywnwyf blyg,
Air hagr o'th gerdd, ŵr hygryg,
Talu a wnaf, leiaf ludd,
Triphwyth o wawd yt, Ruffudd.
Ni bydd yn unfarn arnaf,
O beiwyf hyn, ni bwyf haf,
Na'th ofn, ni thyfaist annerch,
Na'th garu, nes haeddu serch.

Da y gwn, mwynwiw gystlwn Menw,
Ditanu nad wyt unenw
Â MeigenRhys meginrhefr,
Magl bloneg, heb ofeg befr.
Mawl ni bu mal y buost,
'Mogel di fod, mwygl dy fost,
Yn Rhys wyrfarw, rhus arfer,
A las â gwawd, lun als gwêr.

I'r tau dithau, da y deuthum,
Sarhäed fydd; saer hoed fûm.

I'll come to your country, famous for feasting,
though you defy me, you dismal weakling,

I'm the clear winner in a clean encounter,
wherever you live, any time of your choosing,
and I can beat you, you're so full of faults,
here where I dwell, make little doubt of it.
I determined to send you, without any difficulty,
three times their weight, my exchange of wit.
If you would have me alter my estimate
(a firm promise, may I perish in failure),
I won't adore you (your shoulder cold to me)
nor desire your friendship, till you deserve it.

And though you wage grim war against me,
I'll angle for rich rewards in your Anglesey.
As for you, detested north-dweller,
dare just once to descend to the south,
you'll be greeted in turn with the grief you gave,
beaten senseless, a badger in a bag.
I guarantee a testing trial, Griffith,
a dangerous duel, in dead earnest.

My cunning comes from Menw the magician.
I'd consider you no kind of kinsman
to Rhys Meigen, that whistling windbag,
that trap, that lard-ass, that tub of lust.
There's no reward in being his relative,
you can claim no credit in that fine family.
Your wraith of a Rhys, who hardly existed,
was rhymed to death, a spineless waxwork.

And for you, I'm the doom you deserve.
I'll slay you with satire, your coffin's carpenter.

Trafferth mewn Tafarn

Deuthum i ddinas dethol
A'm hardd wreang i'm hôl.
Cain hoywdraul, lle cwyn hydrum,
Cymryd, balch o febyd fûm,
Llety, urddedig ddigawn,
Cyffredin, a gwin a gawn.
Canfod rhiain addfeindeg
Yn y tŷ, f'un enaid teg.
Bwrw yn llwyr, liw haul dwyrain,
Fy mryd ar wyn fy myd main,
Prynu rhost, nid er bostiaw,
A gwin drud, mi a gwen draw.
Gwaraeau a gâr gwŷr ieuainc,
Galw ar fun, ddyn gŵyl, i'r fainc,
A gwledd am anrhydedd mawr
A wnaethom, mwy no neithiawr.
Hustyng, bûm ŵr hy astud,
Dioer yw hyn, deuair o hud.
Gwedy myned, dynged yng,
Y rhwystr gwedy'r hustyng,
Gwneuthur, ni bu segur serch,
Amod dyfod at hoywferch
Pan elai y minteioedd
I gysgu; bun aelddu oedd.

Gwedy cysgu, tru tremyn,
O bawb onid mi a bun,
Ceisiais yn hyfedr fedru
Ar wely'r ferch, alar fu.
Cefais, pan soniais yna,
Gwymp dig, nid oedd gampau da.
Briwais, ni neidiais yn iach,
Y grimog, a gwae'r omach,
Wrth ystlys, ar waith ostler,
Ystôl groch ffôl, goruwch ffêr.
Trewais, drwg fydd tra awydd,

Tavern Trouble

One time I came to a singular town
                    (my faithful squire following on)
a sprightly town, a place to feast.
                        Being Welsh, accustomed to the best,
I lodged myself in a suitably fine
                      public inn, and ordered some wine.
I saw a shapely maiden there
                      in the tavern, my heart's desire,
cast my soul at the rising sun
                      of that slim delightful one.
Just for us two, I ordered a roast
                      and a good wine (not to boast).
Boys try anything. I called to see
                      if the shy girl would sit with me.
I'd only whispered, to be honest,
                      two magic words, before her breast
began to fill with love like mine.
                      When my lucky speech succeeded,
all obstacles melted away.
                      I told the lively lass I'd find
my way to her (her raven hair)
                      once I heard snoring everywhere.

All were asleep. Now to my quest.
                      She and I were wakeful. Best
of my ambitions then entailed
                      reaching her bedside. They all failed.
I started badly, tumbling down,
                      clattering as I hit the ground.
A fallen fool gets to his feet
                      with greater clumsiness than speed.
I rose, but here the pains began.
                      Rising, I caught (poor leg!) my shin
against the edge of a noisy stool
                      where an ostler left it out, the fool.
where it had always been (I paid

Lle y'm rhoed, heb un llam rhwydd,
Mynych dwyll amwyll ymwrdd,
Fy nhalcen wrth ben y bwrdd,
Lle'r oedd cawg yrhawg yn rhydd
A llafar badell efydd.
Syrthio o'r bwrdd, dragwrdd drefn,
A'r ddeudrestl a'r holl ddodrefn.
Rhoi diasbad o'r badell,
I'm hôl y'i clywid ymhell.
Gweiddi, gŵr gorwag oeddwn,
O'r cawg, a chyfarth o'r cŵn.
Haws codi, drygioni drud,
Yn drwsgl nog yn dra esgud.

Dyfod, bu chwedl edifar,
I fyny, Cymry a'm câr,
Lle'r oedd garllaw muroedd mawr
Drisais mewn gwely drewsawr
Yn trafferth am eu triphac,
Hicin a Siencin a Siac.
Syganai'r delff soeg enau,
Aruthr o ddig, wrth y ddau:
'Mae Cymro, taer gyffro twyll,
Yn rhodio yma'n rhydwyll;
Lleidr yw ef, os goddefwn,
'Mogelwch, cedwch rhag hwn.'
Codi o'r ostler niferoedd
I gyd, a chwedl dybryd oedd.
Gygus oeddynt i'm gogylch
Bob naw i'm ceisiaw o'm cylch,
A minnau, hagr wyniau hyll,
Yn tewi yn y tywyll.
Gweddïais, nid gwedd eofn,
Dan gêl, megis dyn ag ofn,
Ac o nerth gweddi gerth gu,
Ac o ras y gwir Iesu,
Cael i minnau, cwlm anun,
Heb sâl, fy henwal fy hun.
Dihengais i, da yng saint,
I Dduw'r archaf faddeuaint.

for my impatience, I'm afraid)
in my stupidity I banged
my forehead on the table end.
There was a basin there, of course,
and a full-bodied bowl of brass,
The table fell, a heavy weight,
both trestles, and the chairs to boot,
the brass bowl sang out after me
so they could hear a mile away.
The basin yelled, my soul went dark,
and all the dogs began to bark.

Rising again, I failed to see
(fellow Welshmen, pity me)
by the wall three Englishmen
lay there in their stinking pen,
each one afraid to lose his pack.
Their names were Dick, Jenkin, Jack.
In clouded accents one of the three
spoke to the others angrily:
"That's a Welshman over there,
plotting mischief. Let's take care.
He'll steal our packs. Don't let him be.
Look out. Stop thief. It's robbery!"
Now the ostler woke them all.
Terrified, I hugged the wall.
Shouting threats, they groped around,
searching every inch of ground.
Haggard, angry, scared to death,
I blessed the dark and held my breath,
mumbling prayers, a fugitive,
to save my abject skin and live.
And as my petty prayers were heard,
by God's good graces, undeterred,
sleepless, mortified, half dead,
without reward I reached my bed.
It's good that saints are close. Perhaps
God will forgive my little lapse.

Yr Adfail

'Tydi, y bwth tinrhwth twn
Rhwng y gweundir a'r gwyndwn,
Gwae a'th weles, dygesynt,
Yn gyfannedd gyntedd gynt,
Ac a'th wŷl heddiw'n friw frig,
Dan dy ais yn dŷ ysig.

A hefyd ger dy hoywfur
Ef a fu ddydd, cerydd cur,
Ynod ydd oedd ddiddanach
Nog yr wyd, y gronglwyd grach,
Pan welais, pefr gludais glod,
Yn dy gongl, un deg yngod,

Forwyn, foneddigfwyn fu,
Hoywdwf yn ymgyhydu,
A braich pob un, cof un fydd,
Yn gwlm amgylch ei gilydd:
Braich meinir, briw awch manod,
Goris clust goreuwas clod,

A'm braich innau, somau syml,
Dan glust asw dyn glwys disyml.
Hawddfyd gan fasw i'th fraswydd,
A heddiw nid ydiw'r dydd.'

'Ys mau gŵyn, gwirswyn gwersyllt,
Am hynt a wnaeth y gwynt gwyllt.
Ystorm o fynwes dwyrain
A wnaeth cur hyd y mur main.
Uchenaid gwynt, gerrynt gawdd,
Y deau a'm didyawdd.'

'Ai'r gwynt a wnaeth helynt hwyr?
Da nithiodd dy do neithwyr.
Hagr y torres dy esyth.

The Ruin

Dafydd: Ah, cottage with your crumbling walls
on the steep slope between mountain and moorland,
how sad you seem to those who found you
a fine venue for friendship and feasting,
and see you now with your broken spine
under shattered rafters, a shadowy remnant.

Yet once, inside your welcoming walls
(a bitter rebuke) I remember the time
when there came from you a kindlier comfort
than you offer now, with your shabby shelter,
since once I saw (how widely I sang her)
deep in her corner, my comely dear.

She was a maid of the finest family,
lithe and lively when cuddled closely,
each arm twining, a girl's true grace-gift,
in answer to mine, linked in a love-knot,
this slim one's slender snow-white arm
under the ear of her young praise-poet.

And my arm too, by a simple device,
at the left ear of my loving lady,
both enlaced (like wildwood embraces),
but that day is done. How different now.

Ruin: The grief is all mine (a bewitched building)
forced to submit to wild winds' fury.
A storm straight from the east country,
havoc heaving my sturdy stonework.
Then with a sigh, the wind (sworn enemy)
wrenched off the tiles from my roof timbers.

Dafydd: So it was wind that caused this commotion?
Only last night it winnowed you wickedly,
a rude ruffian ripping your rafters.

Hudol enbyd yw'r byd byth.
Dy gongl, mau ddeongl ddwyoch,
Gwely ym oedd, nid gwâl moch.

Doe'r oeddud mewn gradd addwyn
Yn glyd uwchben fy myd mwyn.
Hawdd o ddadl, heddiw 'dd ydwyd,
Myn Pedr, heb na chledr na chlwyd.
Amryw bwnc ymwnc amwyll.
Ai hwn yw'r bwth twn bath twyll?'

'Aeth talm o waith y teulu,
Dafydd, â chroes. Da foes fu.'

We live our lives bewildered by witchcraft.
That corner (cause now of double dejection)
was my sleeping place, no smelly pig-pen.

Yesterday, standing in such fine fettle,
you sheltered the head of my dear darling,
honest handiwork. Now (by saint Peter)
the storm has stripped your rafters and roof-tiles.
The world is a whirl of sudden illusions.
What wizard's work destroyed this dwelling?

Ruin: The household served their allotted span,
lie (arms crossed) in coffins, the good days gone.

Y Seren

Digio 'dd wyf am liw ewyn,
Duw a ŵyr meddwl pob dyn.
O daw arnaf o'i chariad,
F'enaid glwys, fyned i'w gwlad,
Pell yw i'm bryd ddirprwyaw
Llatai drud i'w llety draw,
Na rhoi gwerth i wrach, serth swydd,
Orllwyd daer er llateirwydd,

Na dwyn o'm blaen dân-llestri,
Na thyrs cwyr, pan fo hwyr hi,
Dros gysgu y dydd gartref
A rhodio'r nos dros y dref.
Ni'm gwŷl neb, ni'm adnebydd,
Ynfyd wyf, yny fo dydd.

Mi a gaf heb warafun
Rhag didro heno fy hun
Canhwyllau'r Gŵr biau'r byd
I'm hebrwng at em hoywbryd.
Bendith ar enw'r Creawdrner
A wnaeth saeroniaeth y sêr,
Hyd nad oes dim oleuach
No'r seren gron burwen bach.

Cannaid yr uchel geli,
Cannwyll ehwybrbwyll yw hi.
Ni ddifflan pryd y gannwyll,
A'i dwyn ni ellir o dwyll.
Nis diffydd gwynt hynt hydref,
Afrlladen o nen y nef.

Nis bawdd dwfr, llwfr llifeiriaint,
Disgwylwraig, dysgl saig y saint.
Nis cyrraidd lleidr â'i ddwylaw,
Gwaelod cawg y Drindod draw.

The Star

Bewitched by a maiden silver as sea-spray
(God understands, who forgives us our foibles)
I was driven on by my distraction
to seek her at home, this sweet soulmate,
with no desire to devolve the task
on some hired deputy to hie to her dwelling,
or to fee a fever-gripped gossip,
a grizzled grandam as my go-between.

I'll not need my path blazed by pitch-brands
or beeswax torches making noon of midnight.
I'd much prefer to sleep through sunshine,
then run through town in dusky darkness.
None to see me, none to take note of me,
free for all follies until day's dawning.

I'm determined to work unhindered
having in view (as I do each nightfall)
the candles of God, who handles our globe,
to guide me to my glittering jewel.
(All praise to the name of the world's creator,
heaven's shaper, celestial carpenter,
who sees to it there's nothing brighter
than this little star's circlet of light.)

She's the beacon blazing at sky's peak,
a lit candle of crystal clarity,
tallest of tapers, ever elegant.
No sly sneak-thief can steal that loveliness,
no October blast can blow out her flame.
She's a holy host-wafer held aloft.

Creeping flood-water cannot drown her,
this handmaid, serving a holy banquet.
She's safe beyond the grasp of thieves,
nestled deep in heaven's tureen.

Nid gwiw i ddyn o'i gyfair
Ymlid maen mererid Mair.
Golau fydd ymhob ardal,
Goldyn o aur melyn mâl.
Gwir fwcled y goleuni,
Gwalabr haul, gloyw wybr yw hi.
Hi a ddengys ym heb gudd,
Em eurfalch, lle mae Morfudd.

Crist o'r lle y bo a'i diffydd
Ac a'i gyr, nid byr y bydd,
Gosgedd torth gan gyfan gu,
I gysgod wybr i gysgu.

No man on earth should yearn to possess her,
she's Mary's Pearl, placed far above.
She shines her beams on every shire,
a pure sovereign of gleaming gold,
a reliable shield, a true reflection
of the sun's image throned in the sky.
She lets me know, with her jewelled light
the direct means to Morfudd's dwelling.

Christ will come to her, cast his cloak over her,
snuff out her splendour, but no time soon,
this round risen loaf of finest flour.
She slips behind the sky to sleep.

Breichiau Morfudd

Twf y dyn tyfiad Enid,
Â'r tefyll aur, a'm tyf llid;
Tâl moeledd, talm o alaw,
Tëyrnasaidd lariaidd law,
Dyn ŵyl dda ei dyniolaeth
A'i modd, gwell no neb ei maeth.

Ddwylaw mwnwgl dan ddeiloed
Ydd aeth i anghengaeth hoed,
Peth nid oeddwn gynefin,
A chael ymafael â'i min.
Gwanfardd addfwyndwf gwinfaeth
Oeddwn gynt iddi yn gaeth.

Amau bwyll, y mae bellach,
Dawn fu, a rhoi Duw yn fach,
Rhyw gwlm serch, cyd rhygelwyf,
Rhôm, od gwn, rhwymedig wyf.
Manodliw fraich mynudloyw
Morfudd, huan ddeurudd hoyw,
A'm daliawdd, bu hawdd bai hy,
Daldal ynghongl y deildy;

Daliad cwlm o gariad coeth,
Dau arddwrn dyn diweirddoeth.
Da fu hirwen dwf hwyrwar,
Daly i'm cylch dwylaw a'm câr.
Dogn oedd ym, o'm hylym hwyl,
Dewr goler serch dirgelwyl.
Llathr ieuo'r bardd, gem harddlun,
Llai no baich oedd befrfraich bun
Goris clust goreuwas clod,
Gorthorch, ni wnaf ei gwrthod,
Lliw'r calch, yn lle eiry cylchyn –
Llyna rodd da ar wddf dyn –
A roes bun, ac un a'i gŵyr,
Am fwnwgl bardd, em feinwyr.

Morfudd's Arms

A girl formed like shapely Enid
      with the gold glint that draws desire,
      a broad brow, a lily's livery,
      her gestures regal, gentle, restrained.
      A modest girl, and most generous,
beautiful in nature, no-one better.

In our woodland nook, her arms round my neck,
      I found myself eager to enjoy her,
      excitement rising, a rare experience,
      and lip to lip kisses cascading.
      A paltry poet, but a handsome drinker,
this was the moment she took me captive.

Now at length I learned my lesson:
      she was a gift granted by God.
      Some love-knot enlaced us, no escaping it,
      linking us as one for ever.
      With her snow-white arm and such bright charm,
      Morfudd held me, her face flaming.
      Some sins are simple. Tight she held me,
face to face in our forest fastness.

How good that sweet gift, pale slender body,
      her loving hands laced about me,
      knot embrace of eager attachment,
      her twin wrists, her knowing trust.
      A dose to my impetuous wooing,
      this secret girl made a brave love-necklace,
      a yoke for a poet, a pearl pendant,
      a welcome weight, white arms about me.
      Right by the ear of this praise poet,
      reward of a chain, and no refusal.
      Chalk white in color, a snow circle,
      a grand gift for a man's neck.
      That woman wove (only he knows this)
for this singer's throat a slender treasure.

Hydwyll y'm rhwymodd hudawl;
Hoedl i'r fun hudolair fawl
A geidw ym, drefn erddrym draidd,
Fy mwythau yn famaethaidd.
Diofn, dilwfr, eofn dâl,
A du wyf a diofal,
A deufraich fy nyn difrad
I'm cylchyn ym medwlyn mad.

Nid serch i neb f'amherchi,
Delw haul, rhwng ei dwylaw hi.
Wedy cael ymafael mwy,
Wawr euraid – wi o'r aerwy! –
Teg oedd weled mewn rhedyn
Tegau dwf yn tagu dyn.

Meddw oeddwn, mau ddioddef,
Meddwaint rhiain groywfain gref.
Mynwyd fy myd rhag fy mâr,
Mynwyn y'm gwnaeth braich meinwar.
Mynwes gylchyniad mad maith,
Mynwair fuant ym unwaith.

A conjurer casting a cunning net.
　　　　May she live long, that honored charmer,
　　　　who preserves for me only (perfect caresses)
　　　　a foster-mother's friendly magic.
　　　　Free from fear, bold-faced, courageous,
　　　　I could be both somber and carefree
　　　　feeling the arms of this faithful girl
wrapped around me, sweet as mead.

This love of mine needs no apology.
　　　　I was white-hot, a sun in her hands.
　　　　We enticed each other to more embraces,
　　　　that jewel girl (that gold torque necklace)
　　　　What a fine sight, sprawled among ferns,
a choice beauty, choking a bard.

Drunk with delight, tipsy with tenderness,
　　　　with love for a lass so slender and strong,
　　　　this girl I adored, no harm could come from her,
　　　　my nape white from that tight necklace,
　　　　that sensible circle clasping me close.
How well I wore that collar, once.

Y Llwynog

Doe yr oeddwn, dioer eddyl,
Dan y gwŷdd, gwae'r dyn nyw gwŷl,
Gorsefyll dan gyrs Ofydd
Ac aros gwen goris gwŷdd.
Mal 'roeddwn, inseiliwn sail,
Lonyddaf dan lwyn addail —
Gwnaeth ar fy hwyl ym wylaw —
Gwelwn, pan edrychwn draw,
Llun gwrab lle ni garwn,
Llwynog coch, ni châr llên cŵn,
Yn eiste fal dinastwrch
Gair ei ffau ar gwr ei ffwrch.

Anelais rhwng fy nwylaw
Fwa yw, drud a fu draw,
Ar fedr, fal gŵr arfodus,
Ar ael y rhiw, arial rhus —
Arf i redeg ar frodir —
Ei fwrw â saeth ofras hir.
Tynnais, o wyrgais, ergyd
Heb y gern heibio i gyd.
Mau och, aeth fy mwa i
Yn drichnap, annawn drychni.

Llidiais, nid arswydais hyn,
Arth ofidus, wrth fadyn.
Gŵr yw ef a garai iâr,
A choeg edn, a chig adar,
Gŵr ni ddilid gyrn ddolef,
Garw ei lais a'i garol ef.
Gwridog yw ym mlaen grodir,
Gwedd âb ymhlith y gwŷdd ir,

Lluman brain garllaw min bryn,
Llamwr erw, lliw maroryn,
Drych nod brain a phiod ffair,

The Fox

Yesterday, determinedly (by God)
I patrolled eager under trees
(Ovid's leaves), an impatient lad
awaiting my white girl in the wood.
As I stood sentry guarding my post
a willing watcher in that green grove
(her teasing coaxes tears from me),
looking a little further I found
an apelike creature, a rude intrusion:
a red fox, prey to the hounds' prattle,
perched on his rump outside his residence
like a wild boar weirdly obedient.

I balanced my bow between my hands,
my fine yew yearning to shoot far,
and I meant like a smart marksman
to hand him a scare, there on the hilltop—
this fleet spear speeding over the fields—
to aim at him a shapely shaft
straight I drew with dangerous strength
right back, just behind my jawbone,
and suddenly to my dismay
it snapped in three parts, a disaster.

Furious with the fox at first
(that baleful bear), I tamed my temper.
He's the lad who lusts after hens
and feathered fools, who'd relish fresh fowl,
the lad who loathes the huntsman's horn.
His carolling's a crude hound howling,
he's crimson crossing grizzled gravel,
an ape shape in the trees' greenery.

A scarecrow flag on the hill's crest,
he gallops the acres, a glowing ember,
a raven replica, mirror for magpies,

[handwritten annotations: A; woodland setting; intrusion of the natural; I : animal; personified fox: - apelike? - residence - lad lusts after hens; marksman; yew - folklore's superstition; Battle like; races away in front of any hunter's horns; alliteration]

81

Draig unwedd daroganair,
Cynnwr frŷn, cnöwr iâr fras,
Cnu dihareb, cnawd eirias,
Taradr daeargadr dorgau,
Tanllestr ar gwr ffenestr ffau,
Bwa latwm di-drwm draed,
Gefel unwedd gylfinwaed.

Nid hawdd ymy ddilid hwn
A'i dŷ annedd hyd Annwn.
Deugwae'r talwrn lle digwydd,
Delw ci yn adolwg gŵydd.
Rhodiwr coch, rhydaer y'i caid,
Rhedai 'mlaen rhawd ymlyniaid.
Llym ei ruthr, llamwr eithin,
Llewpart a dart yn ei din.

the Red Dragon promised in prophecies,
a prime chaser who gnaws plump chickens,
a famed fleece on fiery flesh,
a drill driven into earth's underbelly,
a lamp's fire in the window-corner,
a coppery longbow, loping quietly,
a pair of pincers, a bloodstained beak.

There was no chance for me to chase him
into his lair there in the underworld.
He can be found both ends of a field,
the ghost of a dog, a danger to geese,
a russet racehorse too quick to be captured,
pacing ahead of the chasing hounds,
a gleam of light, leaping over the gorse,
a leopard dragging a dart in his loins.

[handwritten annotations:]

alliteration

Red Dragon

G7

— echoes of myth Actaeon myth? (where hunter becomes hunted, possibly conflated)

↓ otherworld

hunting

poems draw from welsh legend & traditional verse (Eigr, Tegau, Enid)

p. 8 prince fall in wales

p. 10 waiting for girl in woods only to be interrupted by otherworldly intrusion

attempts to repel fox metamorphose into an enigmatic meditation on his own inefficacy as a lover

— native tradition of elegy & military panegyric & diction that harkened back to 6th c. Gododdin

83

Cyngor y Bioden

A mi'n glaf er mwyn gloywferch
Mewn llwyn yn prydu swyn serch
Ddiwarnawd, pybyrwawd pill,
Ddichwerw wybr, ddechrau Ebrill,
A'r eos ar ir wiail,
A'r fwyalch deg ar fwlch dail,
Bardd coed, mewn trefngoed y trig,
A bronfraith ar ir brenfrig
Cyn y glaw yn canu'n glau
Ar las bancr eurlwys bynciau,

A'r ehedydd, lonydd lais,
Cwcyllwyd edn cu callais,
Yn myned drwy ludded lwyr
Â chywydd i entrych awyr
(O'r noethfaes, adlaes edling,
Yn wysg ei gefn drefn y dring):

Minnau, fardd rhiain feinir,
Yn llawen iawn mewn llwyn ir,
A'r galon fradw yn cadw cof,
A'r enaid yn ir ynof,
Gan addwyned gweled gwŷdd,
Gwaisg nwyf, yn dwyn gwisg newydd,
Ac egin gwin a gwenith
Ar ôl glaw araul a gwlith,
A dail glas ar dâl y glyn
A'r draenwydd yn ir drwynwyn.

Myn y nef, yr oedd hefyd
Y bi, ffelaf edn o'r byd,
Yn adeilad, brad brydferth,
Ym mhengrychedd perfedd perth,
O ddail a phriddgalch, balch borth,
A'i chymar yn ei chymorth.
Syganai'r bi, gyni gŵyn,
Drwynllem falch ar y draenllwyn:

The Magpie's Message

I was sick in love with a splendid lass,
loitered in copses, composing love-songs.
A day dawned with a snatch of satire,
under cloudless skies, early in April,
the nightingale fluting on fresh growth,
the elegant blackbird on emerald battlements,
the wood-thrush on her topmost twig
singing full-throated, ready for rain,
golden quavers on a green quilt.

And the skylark with his subtle song,
sweet soothsayer in his gray cowl,
contemplating that weary climb
with his poem of praise to heaven's height.
(From ploughed field a prince flying,
turning in circles, unwinding upward.)

But I, song-bard of a slender beauty
sat safe and solitary in my green grove,
but moping, my heart haunted by memories,
though truth to tell my spirits soared
from pure pleasure in my woodland wanderings,
enjoying the forest fresh in its finery,
the young shoots of grapevine and wheatstalk,
soon after sun-drenched rain and dew
and the brave greenery on the glen's brow,
the thorn thickets with snow-white nosegays.

And in that place, by God, appeared
a magpie, creation's cunning bird,
building (ambitious architect)
well within the glowering hedge
a clever construction of leaves and lime,
her mate with her, a wise helpmeet.
The magpie muttered her angry indictment,
perched on her thorn throne, nose in the air:

'Mawr yw dy ferw, goegchwerw gân,
Henwr, wrthyd dy hunan.
Gwell yt, myn Mair, air aren,
Gerllaw tân, y gŵr llwyd hen,
Nog yma ymhlith gwlith a glaw
Yn yr irlwyn ar oerlaw.'

'Dydi bi, du yw dy big,
Uffernol edn tra ffyrnig,
Taw â'th sôn, gad fi'n llonydd,
Er mwyn Duw, yma'n y dydd.
Mawrserch ar ddiweirferch dda
A bair ym y berw yma.'

'Ofer i ti, gweini gwŷd,
Llwyd anfalch gleirch lled ynfyd,
Syml a arwydd am swydd serch,
Ymlafar i am loywferch.'

'Mae i tithau, gau gymwy,
Swydd faith a llafur sydd fwy:
Töi nyth fal twyn eithin,
Tew fydd crowyn briwydd crin.
Mae yt blu brithddu, cu cyfan,
Affan a bryd, a phen brân.
Mwtlai wyd di, mae yt liw teg,
Mae yt lys hagr, mae yt lais hygreg,
A phob iaith bybyriaith bell
A ddysgud, breithddu asgell.
Dydi, bi, du yw dy ben,
Cymorth fi, cyd bych cymen,
A gosod gyngor gorau
A wypych i'r mawrnych mau.'

'Nychlyd fardd, ni'th gâr harddfun,
Nid oes yt gyngor ond un:
Dwys iawn fydr, dos yn feudwy,
– Och ŵr mul – ac na châr mwy.'

Magpie: What's all this pother, this paltry poetry,
you old dotard, locked in your loneliness?
You'd be much better, by quick-witted Mary,
to take your gray beard to the chimney corner,
instead of under dewdrop and raindrop
here in the green grove, shivering in showers.

Dafydd: Magpie, you cruel black-beaked bird,
flown out of hell with horrid fury,
hush your hullabaloo, I require quiet,
some serene space as I wait to woo her.
Though it's great love for this loyal girl
that contrives a cauldron where my soul seethes.

Magpie: There's no sense being a slave to passion,
you drivelling gray-haired half-baked dolt.
It's simple folly to seek her friendship,
to lose your mind, however lovely the maiden.

Dafydd: You yourself (impertinent intruder)
have a long labor of your own to honor.
Your nest's no better than a bush of gorse,
a woven basket of broken withies.
Your feathers are speckled and black (worth plucking),
you've a crochety face, a crow's features.
Your coat may be motley, colorful, merry,
but your castle's vile, your voice croaking.
From every fragment of foreign phrases
you've borrowed wisdom on black wingtips.
Magpie, your memory's a dark dungeon.
If you're so clever, dig down cunningly
and allow me now a ready remedy
to cure me of my cruel compulsions.

Magpie: This girl's too dear. She's not for Dafydd.
That's all you need to know from me.
My song is serious. Hide, be a hermit.
You're a luckless man. You must love no more.

Myn fy nghred, gwylied Geli,
O gwelaf nyth byth i'r bi,
Na bydd iddi hi o hyn
Nac wy, dioer, nac ederyn.

Dafydd: I swear to you, in sight of God,
if I ever meet with a magpie's nest
I'll leave it empty of its eggs
by Heaven, and every fledgling I find.

Y Drych

Ni thybiais, ddewrdrais ddirdra,

Na bai deg f'wyneb a da,

Yni syniais yn amlwg

Yn y drych; llyna un drwg!

Yna dywod o'r diwedd

Y drych nad wyf wych o wedd.

Melynu am ail Luned

Y mae'r croen, mawr yw na'm cred.

Gwydr yw'r grudd gwedy'r griddfan,

A chlais melynlliw achlân.

Odid na ellid ellyn

O'r trwyn hir; truan yw hyn.

Pand diriaid bod llygaid llon

Yn dyllau terydr deillion?

A'r ffluwch bengrech ledechwyrth

Bob dyrnaid o'i said a syrth.

The Mirror

Some shocks are sudden.
              I had no notion
my face was not fine
              my features not fetching,
till I felt in my hand
              (such an obvious action)
this mirror—it was
              a dreadful decision.
The mirror told
              the truth of my looks
(I should have known)
              I'm now less than lovely,
made yellow, made sallow
              by a girl full of friendship,
my cheeks like chalk
              a colorless countenance.

After such laments
              my skin's translucent,
a thin lemon-yellow
              an old bruise all over.
My nose is so sharp
              you could easily shave with it
(the shame of showing
              a snout like a razor).
My eyes used to sparkle
              but now, sad to speak of,
they sit blind in my head
              holes bored by an auger.
My locks, once lovely
              with curls in clusters,
now fall out in fistfuls
              ripped from the roots.

Mawr arnaf, naid direidi:

Y mae'r naill, ar fy marn i,

Ai 'mod yn gwufr arddufrych,

Natur drwg, ai nad da'r drych.

Os arnaf, gwn naws hirnwyf,

Y mae'r bai, poed marw y bwyf!

Os ar y drych brych o bryd

Y bu'r bai, wb o'r bywyd!

Lleuad las gron, gwmpas graen,

Llawn o hud, llun ehedfaen,

Hadlyd liw, hudol o dlws,

Hudolion a'i hadeilws.

Breuddwyd o'r modd ebrwydda',

Bradwr oer a brawd i'r iâ,

Ffalstaf, gwir ddifwynaf gwas,

Fflam fo'r drych mingam iawngas!

What's to become of me
                 now I'm not beautiful?
I have two methods
                 to measure my value:
as a dark speckled quiver
                 quite empty of arrowshafts
(with no tried target),
                 or my mirror's a liar.
If my pining's the cause
                 (passion's always a curse)
I'd doubtless be better
                 dead and buried.
If the fault's with the mirror
                 (its mottled features),
then I'm ready to break it
                 be rid of the burden.

It's a round green moon
                 a lustrous compass,
shot through with magic
                 a shining magnet,
a changeable gem
                 a charmed jewel,
made by a magus
                 the work of a warlock,
a dream so fleeting
                 it's fled directly,
a stone-cold traitor
                 ice's half-brother,
a malign liar,
                 a mannerless lad,
may it perish in hell-fire,
                 this loathsome looking-glass.

Ni'm gwnaeth neb yn wynebgrych

Os gwiw coeliaw draw i'r drych,

Onid y ferch o Wynedd;

Yno y gwŷs difwyno gwedd.

How could these furrows
                be found on my features
(if I'm to believe
                what my mirror betrays)?
Charms can change
                a lover's complexion.
They gather that well
                those North Wales girls.

Cystudd Cariad

Curiodd anwadal galon,
Cariad a wnaeth brad i'm bron.
Gynt yr oeddwn, gwn ganclwyf,

Yn oed ieuenctyd a nwyf,
Yn ddilesg, yn ddiddolur,
Yn ddeiliad cariad y cur,
Yn ddenwr gwawd, yn ddinych,
Yn dda'r oed ac yn ddewr wych,
Yn lluniwr berw oferwaith,
Yn llawen iawn, yn llawn iaith,
Yn ddogn o bwynt, yn ddigardd,
Yn ddigri, yn heini'n hardd.

Ac weithian, mae'n fuan fâr,
Edwi 'ddwyf, adwedd afar.

Darfu'r rhyfig a'm digiawdd,
Darfu'r corff, neud arfer cawdd,
Darfu'n llwyr derfyn y llais
A'r campau—dygn y cwympais.
Darfu'r awen am wenferch,
Darfu'r sôn am darfwr serch.
Ni chyfyd ynof, cof cerdd,
Gyngyd llawen nac angerdd,
Na sôn diddan amdanun',
Na serch byth, onis eirch bun.

Love's Affliction

My heart (vile traitor) began to fail, while
passions staged their own rebellion

> In a hundred disappointments
> in the desire of youthful blood
> in a tireless young man's vigor,
> in two wrists fettered by love,
> in scant respect for poetry, robed
> in the shallow bravado of youth,
> in vanity's all-consuming mirror,
> in easy exchange of pleasantries,
> in health enough, a touch of fame,
> in laughter, grace, and elegance.

So now grown old I settle the score,
wrinkled and sad, waiting for death.

> Gone is my old familiar swagger,
> gone that vigor, and that passion,
> gone the rapid rush of language,
> gone my triumphs, and my failures,
> gone my verses made for Morfudd,
> gone dreams of fame, hope of amours,
> gone all memory of my verses,
> gone all jesting, all desire vanished,
> gone those stories boasting of conquests,
> gone all affection. Unless she beckons.

About the Poet

DAFYDD AP GWILYM was the greatest poet of medieval Wales. A brilliant and canny poet of love, Dafydd explores the intensity of erotic desire: its deep seriousness as well as its deep comedy. Born in Cardiganshire around 1320, he was trained in the Welsh bardic tradition and traveled widely throughout Wales. Although distant in time and circumstance, Dafydd's work confronts us with a virtuosic strangeness, a directness, and a sense of lived realness. In his poems, he lingers outside a village, loiters in the woods waiting for a tryst that never happens, peers through a window, stumbles in the dark. Despite the centuries and the technological gulfs that separate us, Dafydd's world is also our world, and his poems, like the best of all poetry, surprisingly modern. With a voice coy, confident, and continually alluring, his poetry beckons and endures.

About the Translators

PAUL MERCHANT was born in Wales and taught for many years at Warwick University. Since 1988 he has lived in Oregon, where he was Director of the William Stafford Archives in Watzek Library at Lewis & Clark College. His volumes from Five Seasons Press include *Bone*  *from a Stag's Heart* (1988 Poetry Book Society Recommendation), *Some Business of Affinity* (2006 Oregon Book Award finalist), and *Bread & Caviar* (2016). His translations from Greek, Modern Greek, Latin and Welsh have been published by Five Seasons, Trask House and Tavern Books.

MICHAEL FALETRA is Professor of English and Humanities at Reed College in Portland, where he specializes in the literatures of medieval Britain. He is the author of *Wales and the Medieval Colonial Imagination* and the translator of Geoffrey of Monmouth's *History of the Kings of Britain.*

Made in the USA
Middletown, DE
22 February 2020